Faith for Ava

My Faith Journey to God's Promise

Faith for Ava

Alexis Prince

Copyright © 2016 by Alexis Prince

All rights reserved. This book or any portion thereof may not be reproduced or used in any manner whatsoever without the express written permission of the publisher except for the use of brief quotations in a book review.

Printed in the United States of America

Edited by Kristen Corrects, Inc.

Cover art and interior design by Heidi Connolly, Harvard Girl Word Services

First edition published 2016

10 9 8 7 6 5 4 3 2 1

Prince, Alexis

Faith for Ava / Alexis Prince

p. cm.

ISBN-13: 978-0-9907590-2-7

Georgetown Literary books may be purchased for educational, business, or sales use. Please contact GeorgetownLiterary.com.

Dedication

To my sweet Ava Pooh, you are the joy of my life. It is you who I love. It is you who I adore. It is you who is the greatest gift to my life. I thank God every day for thinking so highly of me that He would allow me to be your Mom. God told me many years before you were born that you would be great, and it is an honor being able to watch you grow and develop into the greatness that He has called you to be. Continue to be sweet, courageous, beautiful, kind, confident, and generous as God has created you.

I love you, my sweetness!

"Before I formed you in the womb I knew you, before you were born I set you apart." - Jeremiah 1:5 NIV

Acknowledgments

There is a tight-knit group of people who have been instrumental in the birth of *Faith for Ava*. They are my squad. They are the ones who walked the journey of this book with me, all the while encouraging me, supporting me, and comforting me as I opened old wounds and exposed past pains that I thought were tucked away for good. Thank you for seeing in me what I couldn't see for myself. I love you all!

Patricia Ingram—my dear mother, thank you for your unconditional love and support in everything I set out to accomplish. You are my biggest cheerleader! You are my rock! I am who I am because of you. I hope that I make you proud. I love you, Momma, forever and always!

Teddy Ingram—my father, thank you for loving me and always being there for me. You have always been my best listener while always giving me sound advice, always for my good. Anyone who knows me knows that when I say, "Well, Teddy said…." pretty much can be taken as the law. I hope I make you proud.

James Prince—You were one of the first to tell me that I could do it! Thank you for believing in me. Now our precious daughter will be able to read her story in addition to us telling it to her.

Sybrenia Grant—You are a true definition of a sister. The keeper of my secrets. How can I ever repay you for the countless times you have listened to me, cried with me, and told me everything would work out? Thank you for being my "go to girl," the one I can count on to make me smile and feel better.

Tracy Pope—my best friend AND my brother! Who could ever ask for a better combination? You have always unconditionally had my back and that means the world to me. You will never know how many times you have unknowingly boosted my confidence, especially the times that you tell me how smart you think I am. I love you to the moon and back, and back again!

Regina Gibbs—Thank you for speaking life into this book. Thank you for being obedient in God and prophesying over me in regards to this story. I wouldn't have started this journey if it were not for you and your encouraging words.

Shi Evans—To you I owe a standing ovation! Thank you for taking on this project! From day one, you have been so patient with me, while teaching me and walking me through the process. Thank you for allowing me to blindly follow your lead. When God told me it was you who would help me, I knew then that this was going to be special. You have such a gentle spirit, and your love for me has been greater than I have ever known. I am grateful for you! You are the BEST!

Foreword

I told a childhood friend that I wanted to share my testimony. I wanted to share my struggle with infertility and how God blessed me with a miracle I call Ava. My friend naturally asked what the struggle was about exactly. For example, she wanted to know if it was a medical issue. Among other questions, she also wanted to know if I stressed about finding the right partner before Mother Nature had her say. I'm not sure I expected so many questions or expected to delve so deeply into my past.

Then she explained to me that giving my testimony is exactly what she asked me to do. Testimonies do not happen in a vacuum. They often come with a full narrative. In order to bless you all with my testament, I must reveal the complete path I took to receive it. I must let everyone know how I positioned myself to receive the blessings we all ask from God. You may not relate to the blessings I voiced, but everyone asks for a need or desire or yearns for something that at times seems out of reach.

I must admit I am not speaking about a detailed account of events in a court of law. I am talking about an experience that is so much more fulfilling and spiritually sustaining. I am speaking about my Christian testimony. When I speak about my testimony, I talk about how I came to know the God of the Bible through His Holy spirit in my life and in my heart. If I want to share how my miracle came into my life, I have to show the intricate twists and turns my life took. I see now that I must completely show how God's Spirit worked not only during my miracle but that His love and guidance were right there with me throughout my whole life whispering in my ear. To unveil my whole journey, I feel obligated to share the times I did not listen and how He never left my side to prepare me to receive my little miracle—Ava.

The truly amazing part is that I can pinpoint specific events where God worked in my life to lead me to the miracle for which I yearned for so long. I was able to recognize God's intervention in my life because I was taught about God's love and grace as a young girl. Now, some may say that it is not best to force beliefs on children, to let them choose. Contrary to that belief system, I am so thankful I was introduced to God's love at a young age and was able to recognize Him working in my life. Yes, part of my testimony includes Him bringing me out of a difficult situation and how my faith was strengthened because of it. Thankful for all of us, the testimony does not end there. The good news is it continues. He will continue to dwell in us, lead us, and shape us into exactly who we are meant to be.

There were some definite steps I took to become the woman I am today. I had to journey through young adulthood with all of those challenges. Unfortunately, some young adults have more challenges than others and do not make it through those trying years. A lot of us take it for granted that we make mistakes as young adults. Unfortunately, some mistakes cost young people their lives. I am very well aware that I am lucky to make it through those difficult times.

I find it incredible that I can delve even further into my childhood and see how God touched my life. I am so thankful I was introduced to His love as a child and was able to recognize, as a young adult, God working in my life. I have a wonderful family to thank for introducing me to God and encouraging me to nurture my relationship with Him. My parents, sister, and brother are all believers in Christ. However, I must say my mother went above and beyond to ensure I was introduced to Christ and had a personal relationship with Him.

Part I

Getting to Know Him

I call this section "Getting to Know Him" because I want to tell how I came to really know Him, how I came to trust Him, and how I came to love Him. If I am to tell a complete story about my love for Him, I have to show how I was introduced to God and how I had to let go of my plan and trust His plan. I have to admit, my plan had me in an abusive marriage living far away from my family and friends. By telling those aspects of my life, I will reveal how trusting Him placed me in a position to receive the blessing He had in store for me.

For so long, I prayed and prayed for God to bless me with a child. I could not understand why my prayers were not being answered. It was not until I trusted Him and started to follow the path He wanted me to follow that I started to receive blessing after blessing. Depending on one's views, fortunately or unfortunately before the blessing comes the journey. Once my journey is revealed to you, you will wonder why I do not regret any aspect of it. I do not regret any parts of my journey because without it I would not appreciate the sweet life I enjoy today. It would not mean as much or feel as precious. I know I have Jesus to thank for it.

God and the Bible have been intertwined in my life for as long as I can remember. I was raised in the church, as a Southern Baptist Christian. My family and I went to church every Sunday, especially when I was young. I know some children do not like church all that much. They do not like getting dressed up, or they don't like sitting there listening to a man talk about things they don't really understand. However, I must say that getting a piece of gum or candy from my mother's purse made it more bearable. Mostly, I did not mind going to church, especially when we went with our cousins. Meeting up with them always made it fun. They were my partners in crime, if I can say that about church.

The fond memories that I have of my cousins were just hanging out in the back of the church, playing games and telling jokes. After service, we would all go to my grandmother's house for Sunday dinner. We would take a change of clothes so we did not dirty our Sunday best and run around my grandmother's house and yard, continuing the childish shenanigans. It was so much fun. We looked forward to this part of the Sunday routine every week.

One Easter when I was around age seven, my sister and I were on schedule to do an Easter speech in front of the church. We had practiced for weeks, knowing every line, exactly how to stand, and when to smile. I still remember it to this day: *"Why are you looking at me so hard, I didn't come to stay. I just came to let you know today is Easter day."*

The day finally came and at our scheduled time, we both went up and stood in front of the church. We were in position to start, but our mouths would not open. We just stood there looking at the congregation with blank stares. All the while they were staring back at us. We had stage fright. I remember seeing my mother and grandmother motioning for us to start, but we just couldn't. Nothing would come out of our mouths. Finally after quietly standing there for several minutes, we were told to go sit down. I went to sit next to my grandmother, hoping she would tell me everything was okay, like grandmothers usually do. But she didn't. She was so mad. If I was old enough I would have felt indignant. Where was the sympathy for my traumatic experience? She finally said to me, "I am so disappointed in you two. The speech was easy enough for you to do, and you didn't do it. For that, you don't get any peppermint." That was like a dagger in the heart. She always gave us peppermint from her purse at church. Not that day because she was right. The speech was so easy. Today, I'm almost certain my little Ava could say it backward if she was so inclined to do so. There was not a song and dance or anything to make it complicated. All I had to do was stand there and follow my older sister's lead. That is it—it was my sister's fault. My sister and I still laugh about our speaking engagement to this day.

Since I am being honest about my relationship with Christ, I must admit that church felt rather long to me at times. After speaking with friends about our experiences growing up in the church, I am so thankful our church did not meet like other Southern Baptist churches. For example, my childhood friend's church used to celebrate some type of anniversary almost every month. She said they observed the church anniversary, the pastor's anniversary, the missionary board's anniversary, the choir's anniversary, the men's choir anniversary, the senior's choir anniversary, and just about any other anniversary you can imagine. Celebrating an anniversary meant attending regular church service, which was over around 1:30 in the afternoon, followed by a break. The congregants would eat a potluck-style lunch. Then church would resume with a special program recognizing whichever anniversary was on the program. These celebrations usually lasted another two hours. Talk about a long day for a child.

I did not have any negative feelings about church as a child. I thought it was just a way of life. I thought it was something that just about everyone did on Sunday mornings. I thought everyone got up way too early from staying up late on a Saturday night. I assumed most everyone had a hearty breakfast before slipping into their Sunday best. Everybody knows that down South you do not step out to church without putting on your Sunday best.

My mother was no exception. She is known for her style and pizazz. She would settle for no less for her children no matter how tough our financial situation seemed or how many long hours she had to work to ensure we had the best. Even to this day, if anyone attends an event that my mother plans, they know they are in for a treat. If I inherited one-fourth of her style and grace—I cannot go wrong in whatever event I plan or host.

Even though we attended church in our Sunday best looking like angels, church topics can seem somewhat scary to a child. Sometimes the topic is about sin or the devil. When I was a young girl, children's church did not exist, at least at my church. Children sat through the same sermons as the adults. More often than not, the topic was not age-appropriate. For example, pastors teach about topics that range from tithing to adultery.

It was not until I became an adult that I realized some people use fear to teach about God to try and make believers out of those with whom they come in contact. They use fear to keep people in the church as well. It is as if they do not trust that His love alone is enough to touch someone's heart. They do not believe that His love is enough to sustain them. I am so thankful I was introduced to Him through His love and not fear for what would happen if I did not accept Him. I was not afraid of church, or God, or any of the things we were taught as Christians.

I feel compassion for my childhood friend who was taught to fear God. Amazingly she was taught that she could be punished almost instantly for any sin she committed. Can you imagine a child fearing the Hand of God could reach down any minute and mete out some punishment for any indiscretion, whether it is major or insignificant? Again, I am so thankful my mother introduced me to more of God's love and grace than His wrath and judgment. However, I do have a healthy fear of not living by His principle, which stems from believing the typical Christian beliefs that were taught to me.

I suppose I should not say I believed the typical Christian beliefs because there are three large segments of Christianity. There are Catholic Church, the Eastern Orthodox Church, and the numerous, almost too many to count denominations of Protestants. We all know there is nothing like seeing two Christians arguing about whom is right in their belief or quoting scripture trying to prove their point. My family, being Southern Baptist Christians, definitely fits the bill as a Protestant religion. We believe in God the Father. We believe in Jesus Christ as the Son of

God and Holy Spirit. We believe in His death, resurrection, and ascent into Heaven. We believe in communion as a way to cleanse our sins. We strongly believe Jesus Christ's second coming and salvation for those who remain faithful. This all seems straightforward, but even among Christians who believe these tenets, many of us find points to disagree upon or how to apply them to everyday life. One constant exists in Christianity is that believers will find some disagreement about religion. Sadly, we have a testament to the derision among various religions by looking at the countless wars fought in the name of it.

As for me, I cannot remember exactly what I was told about God as a young child, but from what I remember, I thought God was a big person who lived in Heaven and was always looking down and watching us through the clouds. I pictured Him checking to see if we were naughty or nice. Yes, I sort of thought of Him like Santa Claus. If you were good, you would receive His blessings. If you were bad, you would miss out on them. I do not think I really thought I would get punished, but I did not want take any chances and miss my blessing. My rationalization of God was the thinking of a little girl trying to grasp such a magnificent concept.

Therefore, if I had to say I was afraid of anything about God, I was always afraid of disappointing Him. One of my aunts used to always say, "God don't like ugly." So, I would always think, *I do not want God to think I am not being nice* or *I do not want Him to be mad at me.* Fortunately, for my childhood, I do not remember much talk about Hell, the devil, or sin. Thank the Lord my mother taught us to love God with a healthy fear. I think my siblings and I pretty much felt the same way about church. We all grumbled that church was a bit too long, but it was alright when Momma reached into her purse and pulled out some candy. Overall, I liked it okay. I did not have any negative feelings about it. I thought it was just the way of life, something that you did. As a matter of fact, I have fond memories of attending church in my youth, which I am eager to pass on to my child.

One aspect of getting to know Him that I am eager to pass on to Ava is learning the Word. My mother taught Bible verses to my siblings and me. I was not quite sure why I had to learn them. I thought it was something else I had to do because I was told to do so. My mother, being the wise woman that she was, wanted us to be familiar with the Bible. Now that I am an adult and had to call on those verses during times of trial and tribulation, I know she planted seeds in our heart. She planted the Word of God so that we would always have it in good times and in bad. My mother knew that your heart at some point catches up with your muscle memory and then it becomes second nature. I have to be honest and say that I don't know for sure if the scriptures ever helped as a kid, but I know for sure that they have served as constants during confusing times and as anchors during times of struggle in my adult years.

One scripture I learned as a child was Psalm 23. As I child I did not know that the world is filled with fear and anxiety. Some people experience anxiety due to situations they have gone through. Others feel fear when they imagine their futures. Sadly, some people live in fear day to day. Those unlucky enough to be born in developing countries deal with fear on a daily basis. They are afraid they do not have enough food for their children. They cannot gain access to proper medication and vaccines to treat diseases that were supposedly eradicated decades ago. They even fear their fellow villagers, as many of those countries are war-torn. At one low point in my life, I too lived in daily fear.

Fear and anxiety is exactly what Psalm 23 addresses. The beauty of Psalm 23 is that it is actually a song, which I will not ever attempt to sing. Nonetheless it is a beautiful song that touches my heart. I salute those who are talented enough to grace us with such an angelic piece of the Bible. Referring to it as an angelic song is perfect because in Psalm 23 David describes God as his Protector and Provider. Even in my small, child-like mind I related to this verse as God protecting me. Fortunately for me, all I needed protecting from was a monster or two under my bed. I thank the Lord I did not have to deal with some of the issues many of our children face. Our babies suffer through everything from abuse to neglect. I look at my Ava and wonder how anyone could mistreat a child. I hope and pray many of you will join me in saying Psalm 23 for all of the children who have to suffer through such atrocities.

There is one incident from my childhood where I know God protected and provided for me. I was in middle school at the time, only concerned with childish issues. I was not concerned about safety. I just thank God He looked out for me when I was not wise enough to look after myself. I walked home from school that day. I waited to cross the street. My school was located on a major highway in my small town. As with many small towns, it was one of only a few major thoroughfares. As I stood there laughing and playing with my brother, I lost track of just how dangerous the road was for pedestrians. I slipped off of the curb and found myself standing in the road. I was so engrossed in my playful banter with my brother that I took my time stepping back on to the curb. As soon as I stepped onto the curb, a huge truck drove by within inches from running over my leg. I was so shocked that I could not speak. It was an eye-opening moment in my young life. I was almost maimed or worse, hit and killed.

I cannot explain it, but I felt like God protected me. As I could not get the day's amazing event out of my head, I came to the conclusion at the ripe old age of twelve that

God must have something special planned for me. I know now that my interpretation of my blessing that day was quite mature for someone my age. Again, I must credit my mother for planting the seed that I can have a personal relationship with God.

I am the middle child of three, with an older sister and a younger brother. My parents divorced when I was five years old, with my mother raising us as a single parent. Even though my father did not live with us, he initially was actively involved in our lives as children. He was, as my sister affectionately called him, a "Six Flags dad." He was the "fun" parent. While not being much of a disciplinarian, he always made life exciting for us. He took us to Six Flags every year. He bought us new bikes, cool toys, and anything else a kid could desire. Thankfully my mother wanted her children to have a great relationship with their father. Therefore, she never made disparaging remarks regarding him in front of us. I cannot speak for her, but she seemed fine with him being the fun parent. Besides, he did the extra things and activities she was not always able to do because of her budget.

Sadly, my fun parent disappeared (and he took the child support payments with him) at least on a regular basis. My mom took up the slack by working double shifts and lots of overtime. She was already scheduled to work swing shifts at the local plant, so adding double shifts and overtime to it just seemed unbearable. She was hardly home anymore, always working so she could take care of us. When she was home, she was mostly tired or asleep. My sister, being that she was the oldest, would babysit us. She made sure my brother and I ate and did our homework. I missed my Momma so much. I missed her being home and awake, the way life used to be. I remember being so happy on the days that I came home from school and saw her up and awake doing things around the house. I would get so excited that I would just follow her around the house even to the bathroom. I just wanted to be wherever she was. She would ask, "Why do you keep following me?"

I just loved her so much. I knew her work schedule like it was memorized to my heart. So, on the days that I knew she would be home during the school day, I would plan to leave my lunch at home so that I could call her and ask her to bring me lunch at school. She would do it every time. I looked forward to it. Plus, her sandwiches were so much better than any sandwich I could ever make. I missed my Momma so much, I remember thinking, *When I grow up and get married, I'm not going to get divorced. I'm not going to work so much that my kids are home alone most of the day.* My mother, in her own way and strength, made it work. It was not easy, and it was not ideal. It also was not uncommon. Almost everyone that we knew was in the same situation. All of my aunts on both sides of the family, friends of my mom, and even many of my friends from school were all part of divorced, single-parent households. Mothers who held everything together while the father was some place out of pocket was far too common. Where did the women get the strength? Is it innate, something you are born with? Either way, I did not want that life.

I did not want to be divorced with children.

Despite her struggles, my mother could be fun as well, just in a different way. Her ideas of what constituted fun were less extravagant. She took us for ice cream on Sundays, and to the local lakes and parks so that we could play. However, my mother, the disciplinarian, was strict and tough. I don't remember much before the divorce because I was five years old when it happened. I do not believe the divorce hardened her. I think being strict is part of her personality. However, I do believe the stress of divorce can affect how a person parents, causing them to be on edge more than usual.

We had all kinds of rules and regulations. One of her biggest things was having a clean house. It seemed we had to clean the house all the time. We were mopping, scrubbing, and vacuuming so much it seemed like we were the little orphans from the movie *Annie*. If we half-cleaned or incorrectly completed a task, we would have to do it again in the midst of her yelling and screaming. My brother used to call her "The Incredible Hulk." If you took her there, she was definitely going to turn green and burst out of her clothes. We laugh about it now, but it was not too funny living through it. I do not think the stress of several jobs caused her temperament to change. I think that's how she was raised and she simply did what she knew. She always talked about all the chores she and her siblings had to do. She made sure to let us know that we had it easy compared to them. Trying to be Mom and Dad probably exacerbated the situation. I'm sure it is a tremendous job raising three children practically alone.

Contrary to her strictness, my mother was very loving. There was a good balance of love and discipline in our home. She always loved on us, kissed us, and showed motherly affection. Some may say it is ironic for someone so strict to display affection, but she often let us know we were loved. Unfortunately some children do not receive that type of love from their parents. Even though I think that being affectionate is part of my personality, my mother's loving gestures toward us made it is easier for me to express how I'm feeling at any given moment. Expression of love is a wonderful gift she passed on to her children.

Another important aspect of Psalm 23 that speaks to me is, "I shall not want." This verse means God will provide all I need. I believe a lot of us get that confused with what we want and when we want it. I must admit that sometimes "wants" really feel like "needs," especially as a child. I did not understand that part. I really thought when you asked for something, you would get it right then and there. I am getting wiser at discerning between the two. I must credit this enlightenment to experiences and mistakes made along the way.

In my young adult years, I was an average happy-go-lucky person. I moved to Atlanta after high school to go to college. I thoroughly enjoyed the new life that I carved out for myself. The hustle and bustle of the Atlanta metro area lured me in hook, line, and sinker—it was so different from my quaint hometown. There was so much to do and so many places to go. It was like I started to see in color. The people I met were not only from all over the country but from all over the world. I heard accents I had never heard before in Aiken, South Carolina. Almost everyone I met seemed cool and exotic. They were much different than the people I knew back home.

I initially I thought I would go to school, get a degree, and move back home and work at the Savannah River Plant. This plant is a major job supplier in my native community. Anyone who was fortunate enough to get a job there was considered to have made it. That was all I knew. I must admit I was somewhat sheltered, but after my first year in Atlanta, I knew I did not want to return to my small town.

The big city felt so exciting and exhilarating to me. It felt like the city always had something going on at all times. Atlanta was this eighteen-year-old's oyster. I could go to the movies at 1:00 in the morning. I had the opportunity to attend museums and plays, all of which I had never experienced. There were restaurants I had never heard of that represented almost every ethnicity from around the world. I would be remiss if I did not mention the shopping. What young lady wouldn't love great shopping? I even enjoyed venturing out to visit the beautiful parks. This type of exposure was simply not available in my small town, which is of course not the case today. My hometown now offers museums, art exhibits, and lectures along with countless restaurants. During that time of my life I did not appreciate all that small town life has to offer.

Consequently, I fell in love with the new sense of sophistication I felt I acquired living in the city. I gained a novel taste for worldliness by associating with African Americans I met, and they eagerly showed me the ropes. It seems as though every one of my new African American friends came from money. I do not mean the money I imagined earning by working at Savannah River Plant back home. Most of them attended the prestigious Historically Black Colleges and Universities in Atlanta.

The HBCUs I refer to are private institutions. This distinction means that they are much more expensive than the public university I attended. Don't get me wrong—my school was a good school, but it was public nonetheless. What I found even more amazing is that most of the students I met at the HBCUs were not on scholarships or financial aid. Their parents were able to write checks when it came time to pay tuition. I was mesmerized. That was just unheard of to me. Their parents were doctors, lawyers, or had Ph.Ds. My naivetés led me to believe these types of African American families only existed on *The Cosby Show*.

My new friends were down to earth and laid back. They were not pretentious at all, and I knew how to fit in with the crowd. Again, I have to give thanks to my mother for ensuring her children had a sense of savoir-faire. Still, on some level they knew I was unaccustomed to their way of life. They patiently brought me along to things they were used to doing with their families. They exposed me to jazz music. We regularly went to listen to jazz artists, which is still one of my favorites. I frequented plays at the Fox Theatre. I remember attending an Alvin Ailey performance. I was blown away. After this type of exposure, I knew there was no way I would return to my small city.

One friend had the most influence in opening my eyes to the uniqueness of the world. He hailed from the Washington, D.C. metro area. He was in a go-go music band. Go-go music originated in D.C., and it infuses funk, hip-hop, and R&B music styles. It spread across the country and made its way to Atlanta. My friend's band played around the city. I could not believe I got to hang out with the band. These guys knew how to have a good time. However, what was more impressive to me was their ability to maintain a balance of work and play. They were some of the most competitive young people I ever met.

Even though I hung out with my friends, I tried to compete with my friends in the classroom. They all seemed so intelligent with goals for their futures. I felt what many call peer pressure, but it was of the right variety. I always tried to keep my priorities in line. I realized I could have the best of both worlds. I can have lots of fun enjoying and exploring life and remain on task. I really hit my stride with maintaining a balance.

As with any young person sampling new lifestyles and experiences, I started to see new possibilities about life. My views, hopes, and dreams started to expand. I felt that I could have whatever I want. All I had to do was pursue it. My hopes and dreams expanded because it was not as black and white as I originally thought it would be. I thought it was as simple as going to school and moving back home. Now I wanted to go places. I wanted to travel. I wanted to see from where all of these well-to-do families hailed. I wanted to explore the cities that had molded my friends. Maybe I could even move to one of those places. I wanted to spread my wings and see the world.

Unfortunately, spreading my wings did not include all of the lessons my mother taught me. I cannot say that I remember scriptures coming to mind in my young adult life while I discovered this unfamiliar world known as the city. The only thing that I really remember in reference to my religious practices was that I missed going to church. I was not reading my Bible or spending much time with God, but I did have a sense that something was amiss. So, I found a nice church near my college that I would frequent, even if I went by myself. As I lived a young adult lifestyle and made young adult mistakes, I did not feel punishment was looming, but I did repent a lot.

I think that is how God was guiding me. The verse that says "He maketh me lie down in green pastures, He leadeth me beside still water" pertains to this time of my life. While I lived the carefree life of a young adult, God still watched over me as if I were His lamb. He still guided me down His path. From time to time I took a detour and made poor choices. Due to my upbringing, I always had a guilty conscious if I did not do the right thing. Eventually I would ask God to forgive me for whatever transgression was at hand.

In the meantime, I had my life planned as such that I would thoroughly enjoy my twenties. I planned to travel and take full advantage of the excitement of life. In my late twenties, I would get married and have all three of my children by the time I was thirty-five. Then, I would enjoy a happily married life for the rest of my life, like all other married couples. Even after my parents' divorce I still had this view of a fairytale marriage. It was picture perfect.

As far as my plan regarding my spirituality, my relationship with God was not that deep. I remember that I loved God, but I was not doing anything in particular to grow my relationship with Him. I just thought it would come in due time, probably in my fifties or so like I perceived that it happened to everyone. It always seemed to me that middle-aged and older people were always the ones that were so engrossed in their religion and spirituality. I assumed this was a natural progression after the young adult years of a few poor choices and a carefree lifestyle, which I relished.

Sometimes a poor choice included choosing a friend or boyfriend who did not share my value for a relationship with God. Other peoples' religion was not in the forefront of my mind. You just had to be a believer. I think the most important lesson that I learned in my young adult life was to trust your instincts when it comes to people. All people cannot be trusted. Fortunately, if you listen closely, your instincts, heart, and that small still voice will tell you everything you need to know. Like all young adults, I did not always listen to that voice.

Part II

Getting to Trust Him

I call this section "Getting to Trust Him" because after I graduated college, I went through some dark times that required me to trust Him to pull me through. I eventually had to choose whether to drown in my suffering or to trust that God would provide for me and step out on faith. I've heard talk about the "calm before the storm." Well, that is just how I would describe that time of my life when I struck out on my own by deciding to not return home and work at the plant.

By the time I graduated college, I must admit I felt rather confident. I was not listening to any voice, whether that voice was in my head or my mother's. I had a degree under my belt, and I had experienced new and exotic people and places. I was ready to settle into a normal and uneventful existence of focusing on my career for the most part. That is just what I did. I concentrated on advancing my career. I was ready to conquer the world, especially the corporate world. I had such tunnel vision that I did not practice my religion like I would have liked, but I still had it tucked away for times of need.

My job at the time was an accounting specialist or some similar title. I did basic accounting duties like accounts payable and receivable, payroll, and month-end close, among other duties. My life was fairly simple at that time. I worked—full time of course—and went out every now and then on the weekends with my friends. I did not have a lot of boyfriends. I think I probably only had two since college. I was sort of on autopilot. I got up. I went to work. I got together with friends occasionally. None of this included faithfully practicing my religion.

Little did I know that Psalm 23 would again relate to my life. I was still the little lamb some say David refers to when he says, "He maketh me to lie down in the green pastures. He leadeth me beside the still waters." I had a good job that had advancement potential. I had a great apartment in an awesome city with boundless entertainment possibilities. I had great friends from college and new ones I met at work. Life was good. I did not think it could get any better except for the companionship of a special man.

At my job's Christmas party, I met the most charming man I had ever seen. I had no desire for an office romance because I heard the horror stories from such attempts of love at the office. However, he was exceptionally charming. It was our first encounter. He approached me rather confidently and introduced himself. He was full of compliments, which probably should have piqued my warning system. Instead I was receptive to his charms and started to rationalize seeing this new man. Although he worked for the company, he worked out of another office in Nashville. I worked at the corporate office in Atlanta. Eventually, I told myself our dating would not be the same as other office romances. If there were ever a disagreement or breakup, we would not have to see each other and interact every day, right?

Another point I used to rationalize dating him was that his position was not necessarily superior to mine. It was just different. He was in sales. He was a very good salesman, I might add. I know some might say most charmers are very good salesmen. He would have to be to get me to buy into the persona he wanted me to believe. He did very well for himself. He was indeed successful. I'm not saying I was looking for that sort of thing, but it was nice to be wined and dined.

His experience and age allowed him to do things for me that many men my age would not be able to afford. He was ten years older than I. Dating him was my first experience with an older guy of that many years. He was more mature than guys my age, and I felt we were on the same maturity level. I was twenty-seven or twenty-eight at the time. Most of the guys my age were not finished sowing their wild oats and partying every weekend. I was over that era in my life. So was he. I think that was also part of the initial attraction for me. Even though he was ten years older than I was, he never acted like he was teaching me things. He was not controlling either. I heard that older men like to date younger women to have a sense of control. He never tried to treat me as if I was a child. He never treated me as if he needed to show me the world because I was ten years younger. I really do not believe that age was ever a true negative factor in our relationship.

On the positive side, his accomplishments allowed him to take me to exclusive restaurants. We went to jazz concerts, and he treated me like a lady. He continued to dole out the compliments. He made me feel special, like I was the most important person in his life. Even though there were a lot of compliments, dinners, and shows, we still had some deep conversations about life. We talked all of the time about any and everything. Communication was never an issue with us.

I also felt like I could not communicate like this with men my age. We talked about politics sometimes. We seemed to agree there. We talked about religion. He was not very religious or spiritual, but he was a believer. That was enough for me. We even talked about past relationships. That's when I found out he had been married two times before. Sometimes when life throws us a curveball, we ask God, "Why didn't you tell me or warn me?" His two prior marriages at such a young age should have been a red flag. More importantly, why did they end? This revelation was a whisper in my ear that I ignored. Needless to say, I envisioned I would be his last wife.

He confided in me about everything. He even opened up about his prior marriages. Some may expect that some great wrong was revealed about the break-ups of his prior marriages. However, I uncovered nothing more than the usual things that can destroy marriages. He trusted me with every aspect of his life. There were not any unanswered questions. He was very open, and his hopes and dreams were in line with mine. We wanted to travel, enjoy life, and build our family. It was very simple after falling in love so quickly. I threw caution to the wind after he swept me off my feet. He was so kind and romantic. It just seemed different and better than any experience than I ever had with other men. He seemed like the perfect guy.

But we all know no one is perfect. As time passed, I started to realize my new love was no exception to the rule.

Behind the façade, I slowly got to know another side of him. There was an angry person lurking behind the charm that peeked out every now and then. At first I noticed it in simple outbursts. For example, whenever we drove to one of our outings I prayed no one would cut him off in traffic. Even the mildest traffic infraction against him would send him into the rage of a madman. Yes, this included vulgar language and that ugly finger people tend to use in traffic. Sadly, ninety-nine percent of the time, that type of reaction with cursing and F-bombs was not warranted. I also noticed seemingly out-of-place angry comments. I often thought he should not act so upset over the pettiest incidents. His anger was not yet directed at me. Therefore, I let it ride.

Strangely, just as quickly as he got angry, he could go back to Mr. Nice Guy. These were clear signs of a deeper issue, but I wanted to believe in the love story that was emerging between us. We developed a long-distance relationship. You would think time apart would leave little room for angry outbursts. You would think when a couple got together, there would be little to disagree about. Maybe it was the stress of dating long-distance that put strain on the relationship. At least that is how I rationalized some of the outbursts. Unsurprisingly, after several months of long distance dating, he asked me to move to Nashville with him. I was ready for a change from the quickly growing and busy Atlanta scene, so I jumped at the chance to see where this relationship could go.

We got serious enough that I wanted my family to meet him. When my family first met him, they thought he was a nice guy. He was very charismatic, smart, and extremely engaging. He was the life of the party. He always had us laughing with jokes he probably had prepared for every occasion. But after spending more time with him, my family thought he was a little snobbish and arrogant. While he charmed my family, he could not help boasting about himself. He was eager to tell them how great he was at this and how great he was at that. He could not leave out the fabulous trips and interesting people he knew. Looking back on the relationship, I have to admit they were right. He was very arrogant and full of himself. However, at the time I saw it as confidence and self-assuredness. His arrogance is what allowed him to approach me at the Christmas party, and it is what drew me into his world.

The fact that he introduced me to his family rather quickly added to the seriousness of our relationship. I felt as if they loved me, and I loved them. They were really sweet people, and I still think about them every so often. His mom is a really sweet woman. His two sisters were always very kind and welcoming to me. His relationship was fine with all of them, especially his mother. Their closeness was evident by how often they used to speak with each other. His relationship with his father was strained for several years and was just getting back on track when I came into the picture.

I noticed that whenever he spoke about his father or when we were around him, there was a lot of tension between the two. He had a lot of anger toward his dad. He'd said his dad was verbally abusive to him when he was young.

I just remember thinking, *He needs me.* I felt I needed to nurture and love him, and he would be fine. I guess I was wrong. Looking back on that time of my life, I do not think he used it to gain pity from me. I think that he told me about the complicated relationship with his father just as a part of sharing as committed couples do. I do not know if he knew it or not, but he played right into my nature of wanting to fix things. I'm a fixer, so I saw an issue and tried to come up with a solution. I could love him through it.

I guess my family was able to tolerate me dating him long distance, but when I decided to move to Nashville they were not happy, especially my mom. She voiced her concerns to me. She said, "There is just something about him that I do not like and do not trust." I couldn't believe what I heard. I couldn't believe I did not have their support. If anyone in my family voiced their concern, I would say to them, "Nobody is perfect. Let me live my life and make my own mistakes." I had no earthly idea how bad a mistake I was about to make. Nonetheless, I at least wanted to try living with my boyfriend.

There was a female acquaintance on the job who pulled me to the side. She said, "I don't know, Alexis, it's just something about him that's not right." I asked her why she would say such a thing. She did not have an answer for me. That is just what I wanted to hear…nothing. I assumed she liked him or was envious because he was a cutie, and many of the ladies around the office liked him. However, it didn't really matter what anyone said. I needed to make my own choices. Making my own choices meant a move to Nashville.

I set out to start a new life with my boyfriend. The move was uneventful. It was fine. He moved all of my things from Atlanta to Nashville. He was very welcoming. He rented a house for us. He lived in a rural area before, but I was not interested in living in a rural area—I wanted to live near the city—and he graciously found a house near the city for us.

As soon as I moved to Nashville, within a week, that ugly monster started showing up. At that point, it was just arguments all of the time. This is where I would say his controlling nature showed up and with a vengeance. One argument I distinctly remember is his anger about me exploring the city without him. I simply tried to familiarize myself with my new town. I like exploring on my own and saw no problem with it. Somehow, I got accused of cheating on him. I would assure him by reminding him that I did not know anyone in Nashville. Sadly, that did not matter to him.

Since I had seen many arguments before between my mother and stepfather, I thought it was normal and I could handle that. I could easily go toe to toe with him, no problem. Then, he slowly started creeping in the verbal abuse. He often told me that I was just a country girl. He told me I did not know anything about the real world. My boyfriend, this fellow man of African descent, told me that my ancestors and I were just "house niggers." I assume he said such horrid things because we were Southerners. He felt superior somehow because he was West Indian. He felt they are much more politically progressive than we are. I thought about the countless Southern African American political activists who marched, held sit-ins, protested, and were beaten or died for his right to have such views.

Those comments were another red flag I ignored. Some might say his comments were not a whisper. They were two hands shaking my shoulders that should have brought me to my senses. I had just moved to a new city and left my old job. I did not feel I could leave just yet. Like anyone trying to see what they can get away with, the insults got worse and worse. They escalated to the level of verbal abuse, something that was weird for me, because I had not dealt with it before in any personal relationship. I did not realize it at the time, but Psalm 23 was right there in my new home. "Yea, though I walk through the valley of the shadow of death, I will fear no evil." I know this verse sounds pretty ominous and some might say my applying it my situation is over the top. I wish I could say applying this verse to my life at that time is an exaggeration, but too many women have lost their lives to physical abuse. Looking back on my situation, I am blessed to be here today to share my testimony. Somehow, I did not have a healthy fear of how badly verbal abuse could get and how it often escalates to physical abuse.

Verbal abuse was so foreign to me. Like I said, I had not dealt with it in my life. People often think they know how they will react in certain situations, but I am here to say from experience: You never know until you are actually in the middle of the storm. Besides, at that point of our relationship, I knew his full story. He revealed the abuse he suffered at the hands of his father. Like many survivors of abuse, he still carried pinned-up anger and pain. This is what I believed caused him to lash out. I felt I understood him. I believed I could help him. I felt I could love him through it.

Despite the verbal abuse, we trudged along with our relationship. I was determined to make it work. We had gotten engaged just before I moved to Nashville—I wanted that type of commitment before leaving my job, home, and friends. He was fine with my stipulation. There was no special, grand gesture for the engagement, which is surprising considering he was so romantic. He did not get down on one knee or anything like that. We both knew we planned to get married in a year after I moved to Nashville. This commitment especially convinced me to stay despite him ratcheting up the abuse and work it out for us.

The arguments got worse and worse. One of his ways of apologizing was to take me on trips. He loved to travel, and so did I. Consequently, I was always ready to go. After a big argument, he would say, "Close your eyes and point on the map." Wherever my finger landed, that is where we would go. He used to say, "Just book the flight." Needless to say, we traveled somewhere at least every two or three months.

But after the wedding is when things really changed for the worse. That's when the verbal abuse went to another level and the physical abuse began. I truly did not know what I had gotten myself into. To make matters more complicated, four to six months after the wedding, I was pregnant.

If I back up a bit, along the way I did tell my mom and my sister about the abuse. We are all very close, so I was and still am very comfortable talking to them about anything, even if it is a touchy subject. They have always given sound advice and have never judged me or made me feel badly for any of the mistakes that I made in life. With that being said, I used to call home and tell them everything, all the time. I told them so much. They did not like him anymore, but I was not ready to leave yet. When things were well again in the house, I wanted them to still like him as I did. I wanted them to be mad when I was mad and be happy when I was happy. But, it does not work that way. Once your family knows when a person has hurt the one they love, it is hard for them to bounce back. They did not like him anymore, pure and simple.

I remember once I called my sister crying because we had a pretty serious fight. At the end of the conversation she said, "Pack your stuff. I'm coming to get you." I did not really believe her, but the next day she was at my front door ready to pack me up. She drove from Augusta, GA to Nashville to see about her baby sister. It's a six-hour drive. I did not know what to do because once again I was not really ready to go. I just apologized for her driving so far with the kids. They were mere toddlers at the time, babies really. On the flip side, I was so happy to see them and to break up the unhappiness in my life.

Besides, I thought I could deal with it because it did not seem to be any different than what other couples that I knew went through. I come from a family of strong women who voice their opinions. I often witnessed couples "going off" on each other. That was normal behavior to me. So, no one could say something sassy or disrespectful to me without me saying something just as sassy or even worse in return. With that being said, I take responsibility for my part to play in the demise of our relationship. Like most violent relationships, every fight we had got worse. The altercations went from simple shoving to punching and dragging. That's when I knew it was really bad, and that I would not be able to stand it much longer.

Coincidentally, my mom was abused by my father. The abuse ultimately drove them to divorce. She always preached to me and my sister to never ever let a man put his hands on us. She had already been through it, and she did not want to see her daughters live a life of fear and violence. She always said, "If a man feels like he wants to hit you, he could just bring you back home where he found you." Although my mom was always in my ear, in the beginning I still wanted to make it work. I did not want to be divorced. I did not want to be like everybody else who got divorced. I did not want to give up on my marriage. I would try to do everything in my power to keep him happy and stable. I thought if he could keep his emotions on an even keel, then he would not get so full of rage. If his mood remained level, then life with him would not be so bad.

As the fights got worse, I felt like I was losing him to the rage. I could not do it. I could not help him, even as his wife. I wanted out of this impossible situation, but I didn't know how. I used to go through the Bible every day desperately searching for a reason to get divorced. I wanted to do things the right way. The best way for me to find guidance has always been to go to the Bible. I am a Christian who was raised in the church. I was taught that the Bible is the blueprint for how to get through life's difficulties. So, what better place is there to go?

In my searching of the Bible, the only clear and concise reason to get a divorce was infidelity. Well, that did not apply to me because my husband never cheated on me.

I was lost. My sister used to always tell me, "God doesn't want His children to be hurt and beat down. He loves you that much." As things progressed, it looked like that was going to be my reason. If I were to ever leave, that was going to be my legitimate reason for divorce. God loves me, and He wants better for me. My sister said she would support me on whatever decision I chose to make.

Back to the one bright spot in my life: my first pregnancy. It was supposed to be a happy occasion. We were so excited. It was our first child in our new life together. We celebrated like any newly expecting couple. We were over the moon. We were not fighting heavily when I first got pregnant. It was mostly verbal, and maybe one or two physical altercations at the time. During the period of time of my first pregnancy, we were in a good place, for us.

I started going to my doctor immediately and all seemed well. All of my levels were high and there were not any signs of anything being wrong. For my eight-week visit, we were supposed to be able to listen to the heartbeat. The doctor could hear it, but he could not see the heart moving on the ultrasound. He and the nurse were baffled. The doctor kept saying, "I can hear it, but I can't see it." He even let me hear it. It was such a strong heartbeat. At first he said, "The baby is playing hide-and-seek." After a while, the doctor decided to send me for a scan of my abdomen to see where the heartbeat was coming from. Low and behold, the baby was in one of my tubes. I had a tubal pregnancy. He and the nurses kept asking me, "Do you feel okay? Are you in any pain? Have you had any bleeding?" My answers were no to everything. I felt fine. I was not in any pain. I did not have any bleeding. Upon more research, my tube was still in tact. It had not burst, and the baby was beautifully growing there. It had made its home there in my fallopian tube.

The doctors informed me of the ramifications of a tubal pregnancy. A tubal pregnancy includes the tube bursting and me losing my life from losing too much blood. My husband was not at this appointment with me. They had me call him immediately. When he came to the hospital, which was in all of fifteen minutes, they told us that they wanted to admit me to the hospital for surgery and remove the baby. I was shocked and horrified. It all happened too quickly. This happened on a Friday. The doctors said that I would not make it through the weekend without this situation going south.

We decided to go ahead with the surgery. We were both saddened and disappointed. I was in shock, so much so that I did not even remember to call my mom, sister, or anyone in my family.

I woke up later that evening in the hospital and the surgery had been successfully performed. Unfortunately, I lost my tube as they were not able to save it, but other than that the surgery was successful. I was happy to be alive, but I was so saddened by this whole ordeal. It was then that we called my family.

I stayed in the hospital over the weekend, and on Saturday the doctor came to check on me. I was only partially awake, as I was on pain medication. I was lucid enough to hear the doctor wanted to talk about something specific. He had ultrasound pictures in his hand, and he wanted to show my former husband and I what they found while performing the surgery.

My uterus was completely covered in fibroid tumors. Per his diagnosis, I would not be able to ever carry a child to term. This was a devastating diagnosis. Even though I was in and out of sleep, I understood exactly what the doctor said. I tried to block it out, and I then let my husband respond to him. My husband vehemently denied what the doctor said.

The doctor was about to receive one of my husband's outbursts. My husband grabbed the ultrasound photos, balled them up, and threw them away. I should not have been shocked, but I was. I started to pretend that I was asleep because I could not take any more drama. Not only did I just lose my first child to a tubal pregnancy, I also found out I had fibroid tumors and I would not be able to have a baby. I was spent.

Later on, I asked my husband what the doctor said, and he replied, "Nothing." He tried to convince me that I imagined the whole conversation between the doctor and him and there were never any ultrasound pictures. Why was he doing that? Was it he who did not want to come to reality? Did he block it out? Even until the last time we discussed it, he said the conversation with the doctor did not occur.

Of course, I found out later at a follow-up visit that the conversation did actually happen. About a year later, I was pregnant for the second time. I knew I was pregnant, but I wanted to wait a couple of weeks before running to the doctor as I did before. I wanted to wait until I was six to eight weeks, so I made my appointment for then. About a week later, I noticed that I was bleeding and it would not stop. I called my mom and explained to her everything I was going through and she suggested I sit or lie down. She said to have my husband take me to the hospital. I asked him to take me to the hospital because I thought I was having a miscarriage. He said to me, "You are not pregnant, and you are not having a miscarriage. I'm not taking you to the hospital." I was dumbfounded. I just started crying, went to my room to rest, and just let *it* happen. I did not want to go to the hospital by myself, I'm not sure why. I'm sure I was afraid, but I may have been ashamed that my husband was not supportive of me.

Sadly, it was all over by the next day. I went to the doctor the next week, and they confirmed that I lost another pregnancy by checking my levels.

I told my husband that I had indeed been pregnant. He didn't really say much. He was sorry that I had miscarried, but I don't remember him apologizing for not believing me. I think I coped by just getting back involved in life. I jumped back into my job, concentrating on that and my hobbies. I used to sew a lot and I also enjoyed house decorating.

A couple of months later, I was pregnant again. Same thing happened just like the last. I miscarried at home. Went to the doctor later and they confirmed our loss.

Several days later, I was home alone, standing in the guest bedroom of my Nashville home profusely crying because once again I miscarried another baby. This was the third time within a year. I was crying and simultaneously asking God, *Why? Why? Why?* Why was I not able to carry a child? I was in an unhappy marriage for a year and a half with seemingly no way out. I felt that if I could have a child, the marriage would be more tolerable. I felt there was not a valid reason at the time to get divorced. I had grown out of love—and like, for that matter—for my husband. There had been so many divorces in my family: parents, aunts, uncles, and cousins. I wanted to try and beat the odds. Hopefully things would get better.

While I was standing there, questioning God of His decisions on my life, I heard Him say to me, *I'm not going to give you a child with him, but when I do, it will be great.* It was not Him speaking to me in an audible voice that everyone could hear—it was in my spirit. It was a small, still voice. I heard it and I felt it in my whole being, body, and soul. It was my first time I heard the Lord speak to me.

In the past I've heard people say, "The Lord told me this. The Lord told me that." Strangely, for someone who believed in God, I had never experienced it. I did not really understand it. When I asked people who professed that the Lord spoke to them how they knew, they would always say, "It's one of those things when you know that you know that you know." Well, I knew it was Him speaking to my heart. I knew it was real. Thou art with me. Thy rod and thy staff they comfort me. God was still with me. I was not alone.

After I heard Him and realized the voice I heard was

God, He stopped talking. That is all He said to me. I was like, "Wait! Wait! What do you mean? Are You saying You are going to give me a child? Is it going to be a boy or a girl? 'Great'? Great how? Doctor? Lawyer? If You are not going to give me a child with him, then who will it be with? And most importantly, are You saying that You are going to release me from this marriage?" I had so many questions, but God was silent. He did not say any more. He did not have to. I now had hope. He was in fact, going to give me a child, and the child was going to be great.

A couple of months later, I was pregnant again for the fourth time. My pregnancy was during the Christmas season. We had planned to go to Kissimmee, FL to spend the holiday with my grandmother and all of my side of the family. As soon as we arrived, I started bleeding. My mom was there, so I informed her of what was happening. I was so relieved she was there. She had me lie down for the rest of the day with my feet up. My grandmother lived in a golf course community with her house on the golf course. My husband loved playing golf, so every day he was out there playing eighteen holes. This particular day, I told him I thought I was miscarrying again. He matter-of-factly said, "No. You are not." Just like that he went to play golf anyway. I called him a couple of hours in the game asking to him to come back because I did not feel well. He nonchalantly replied, "You'll be okay. I want to finish my game."

I was too embarrassed in front of my family to make a big deal of it. I let it be. I miscarried just like the times before. After the vacation was over, I went to the doctor, and they yet again confirmed my miscarriage.

My marriage started to completely fall apart, and quickly. As it turns out, my first marriage was not all that I had hoped and dreamed of for myself. It crumbled like a building falling after being demolished, quickly and unstoppable. I had dreamed of marrying a great guy who embodied all of the characteristics of a young girl's prince charming. He was partially that guy, but not completely. Don't get me wrong—when it was good, it was really good. But when it was bad, it was really bad. Every situation was so extreme. There was never a middle ground. He had a rage that the charming side of him tried to keep at bay but often failed. He would get so angry sometimes that I often took the brunt of the anger, literally and figuratively.

About three weeks after the Christmas in Kissimmee, we had the biggest physical fight of our marriage. Before that awful fight, it seemed like all would be well for a couple of months, and then he would flip out. We would fight. He would apologize in a huge way, and then all would be well again. It was a vicious cycle, and I was finally tired of riding his hamster wheel.

Part III

Obeying Him

I had one last vicious fight with my former husband. Again, it was the worst one we had so far. We yelled and screamed. The fight immediately escalated to the next level. He pushed me and I fell against the buffet table in the dining room and almost hit my head on one of the sharp edges. He picked me up and threw me on the couch. He kneeled over me and punched me so many times that I lost count. He dragged me by my hair from one end of the house to the other end while kicking and hitting me. While all of this was going on, I prayed, *God, if you get me out of this alive, I promise you that I will leave tonight*. This was not one of those promises many of us have to God to help us feel better after too much to drink—you know, the one about vowing to never have another drink if He will make the pain go away. I knew I had to leave or I would end up dead.

When the fight was over, I went to the bathroom to look in the mirror to see how terrible I looked. Miraculously, there was not a scar to be found on my body—no blood or anything. Nonetheless, I was completely sore like I had been working out all day, and my hair was crazy. I guess that was the girl in me looking at my hair during such a horrid situation. When I realized that the Lord had saved me, I remember looking in the mirror and smiling, and I said to myself, *I'm outta here.*

I boldly told him that I was leaving him. He did not process what I told him well at all. He took all of the money and credit cards out of my purse. He even took the luggage so I could not use it. I did not care. I just put my clothes in a trash bag and got in my car to drive home to my mom's house, which was six hours away. When I got in the car, I realized that I only had a small amount of gas. I said to myself, *That's okay. I'll go as far as I can go, and God will figure out the rest.* Then I drove off. I drove and drove and drove. I cannot tell you to this day how I made it to my mom's house. From what I remember, the gas needle hardly moved, and I never stopped for gas. By the grace of God, I made it all the way to my mom's house in Georgia, a neighboring state.

I escaped to safety at my mother's house. I got a job at a major airline company and started to rebuild my life. When my insurance benefits started, I decided to go and have a thorough exam and find the true cause of all of the miscarriages. The diagnosis was in fact fibroid tumors. There were so many of them that they covered the entire circumference of my uterus. Fibroids were the culprit to my miscarriages—there was no place for the egg to implant.

I am so thankful my new doctor suggested a procedure to remove the fibroids, a myomectomy. This entailed a literal scraping of my uterus to remove the fibroids. I cannot come up with an answer as to why this type of exam was not suggested by my previous doctor. I eagerly consented and the surgery was successful.

I was slowly getting my life back to normal. I even tried dipping my toe into the dating pool again. While still working at a major airline company in Atlanta, I befriended a coworker, Evelyn, who for whatever reason had taken a strong interest in my love life. Every Monday morning she would question me about my weekend and any possible dates. None of the dates worked out, so she would always end the conversation with a sigh and say, "We have to find you a nice guy. You are too sweet to be single." I would just smile. Evelyn was so sweet and caring. She did not know anyone at the time, but was determined that there was someone, somewhere out there for me.

After several weeks, she called me and said she thought she had the perfect guy for me. She had just met him the previous day at a company meeting. His name was James. I just laughed and listened to her as she described this perfect guy. She wanted to set us up on a blind date, but I did not want to do that. I told her that the only way that I would meet him is if she came along with me. We compromised, and she set up a meeting in his office for the next Friday. She kept her word and walked with me to his office. I should have known there was going to be something to it because the night before I was supposed to meet him, I started getting really nervous—I mean, sweaty palms and the whole nine! I could not figure out what was happening because I had never been nervous about a guy before.

The next day, Evelyn escorted me to my prince's office as scheduled. James Prince was so handsome as he sat on the other side of his desk with the most beautiful smile I had ever seen. We talked and talked and talked. Since our meeting was in the morning, he asked me out for lunch that day. After lunch, he then asked me out for a real date for the next evening, which was Saturday. I remained nervous and jittery the whole time, and I found out later he was just as nervous.

James and I heavily dated for the next four months. Surprisingly, I did not have an issue with trust. My past marriage was just that…in the past. I was all in now. I adored him, and he adored me. He was always so sweet and romantic to me. Almost every weekend, he had something romantic planned. For our first Christmas together, he took me to New York City for a beautiful holiday. He had everything planned from candlelit dinners, to ice skating at Rockefeller Center, to intimate walks in Central Park. As we were walking in Central Park, he stopped, put his hands in the air and yelled, "I love this woman!" I just blushed the whole time. I was elated. I was in love.

The next month, in January, James planned another big day for my birthday. He would not let me in on his secret. He told me to prepare by packing an overnight bag with something to wear for a nice dinner. I had no idea where we were going. He pulled up in front of a well-known spa. He said, "You have reservations in there. Take your bag and go inside, and I will pick you up when you are finished." I obliged.

When I walked in, everyone knew my name. They said things like, "Welcome Alexis, we have been waiting for you." I kept a big smile on my face, of course, while I wondered what was going on with this surprise. I quickly learned that I had a half-day at the spa complete with massage, facial, mani-pedi, and light lunch. I felt like a princess. I could not believe he had done all of this for me.

After all was complete, the attendant who had been managing my stay told me that I should change clothes into the fancy dress that I had packed. I thought, *How does she know what I have packed in my bag? What in the world does James have planned?*

When I walked outside, James was there waiting, just as he said he would. He was nicely dressed in a dinner jacket and just as handsome as ever. I was smitten all over again. I blushed and grinned and blushed some more. I asked him what was next on the agenda. He told me I'd see when we get there. I just sat back and enjoyed the ride to what I surmised was going to be an enjoyable night. We pulled up to a swanky hotel in downtown Atlanta. As he gave the car keys to the valet, I figured out we had dinner reservations. We walked in and once again, everyone knew our names. They said, "Welcome, Mr. Prince and Happy Birthday Alexis." Our table was scattered with rose petals. I was about to burst with excitement.

After the romantic dinner, the waitress came by and asked if we wanted to take a tour of the museum of the hotel because the hotel had a lot of history. I really did not want to but I agreed—after all, they had been so kind to us. After we walked to the first closed-off area, the waitress said that she had to run and get something and would be right back. I turned around to say something to James and low and behold he was down on one knee with a little red box in his hand. I looked down at him and he popped the question.

I was speechless. I think I just stood there for a few seconds just shocked. I did not have to think about it. I already knew that I would marry him in a heartbeat if he asked me. "Yes, yes, yes I will marry you!" I squealed. After we walked out of the room, the staff greeted us with champagne and congratulations.

On the next level below the restaurant, there was a lounge area where a jazz pianist played and an area for people to sit and listen. James asked me if I wanted to go down there for a few minutes before we left. I thought, *How romantic* and then I said yes.

As we walked down the spiral staircase leading to the jazz lounge, I looked around and I thought I saw some people that resembled my family members. I thought, *What a coincidence.* When we arrived downstairs, the group of people yelled "Congratulations!" The group *was* all of my family—my mother, my brother, two of my sisters, and some friends. James had planned this whole night several weeks prior and everyone was in on it. Unbeknownst to me, he drove to my hometown a couple of days prior and asked my parents for my hand in marriage. After they said yes, of course, he invited everyone to the celebration after the dinner. I couldn't believe that they all knew and no one managed to slip and tell me the big secret. What an amazing night. It was perfect. It is still one of the best nights of my life. Eight months after that, we were married.

"Thou preparest a table before me in the presence of mine enemies: thou anointest my head with oil; my cup runneth over." I have to say the Psalm my mother taught me as a young girl was relevant again. No, my former spouse was nowhere to witness my newfound happiness. However, in spite of everything I went through in that marriage, here I was again in love and marrying the man of my dreams. To make the occasion even sweeter, I had my family there cheering me on with their full blessing. My cup truly runneth over.

Approximately one year after we were married, I realized that my job had a substantial benefit for in-vitro fertilization. I had already informed him about my history with miscarriages. After talking it over with my husband, we decided to try it. The doctor reviewed my health records. She advised me that due to a prior procedure, the lining of my uterus was too thin to carry a child. I initially thought of it as another heartbreak until I remembered what God had whispered to me. I told my husband God said He was going to do it, so I wanted to try in spite of what the doctor was saying. That is exactly what we did.

The first step of the process was ovulation induction. This entailed administering medication to enhance the ovaries. The doctor prescribed a medicine that causes one to release hormones needed to stimulate ovulation. After the first couple of days of being on the medicine, I felt like I was having supercharged PMS. I was so emotional, crying for no reason and getting angry at any little thing. My emotional roller coaster was a lot for my husband to endure. After a week, I went back for my check-up. While waiting in the observation room and being so emotional, I decided I did not want to go through with the process anymore. I did not want to feel the way I was feeling anymore. I did not want to force this process. If God said He was going to do it, then I should just let Him do it and not get in His way. I called my husband and asked him if he was okay with me walking out. He supported my decision. So I walked out and never looked back.

About a year later, I was pregnant. We were ecstatic. Immediately I thought, *I knew God told me that He was going to do it.* I was elated to say the least. Everything seemed to be going well. I made it to my first appointment at six weeks without any issues. The visit was great; everything looked good. I was so optimistic. The next visit we expected to see the actual heartbeat. I had been down this road before, but this time was different. After all, we saw the baby on the ultrasound. He was not hiding this time. *What could go wrong?* I thought.

During the ultrasound, I noticed the technician seemed to search but did not say a word. She had a perplexed look on her face. She left to get the doctor. My heart dropped. I knew something was wrong. The doctor came in and did the same processes as the technician, but he knew what caused the confusion. He explained to us that the baby's heart stopped beating. I was devastated. I could not believe that this was happening again. It was especially hard to digest because I knew what God had whispered in my ear.

My devastation turned to anger. I was so angry with God. Why was He doing this to me? I decided to wait and let my body pass the embryo after the doctor gave the choice of whether to have a D&C or not. I went on for weeks. Still, no embryo passed. The baby was still there, attached. My body seemed to not want to pass it. During that time I was hoping for a miracle. I wanted the doctor to be wrong. I needed her to be wrong.

Reality set in. I waited about three weeks before I decided to have the D&C. There was not going to be a miracle. The pregnancy was not viable. There was not going to be a baby.

After the surgery, I lay in bed in the fetal position and cried all the time for weeks. I asked God, *Why? Why? Why?* I didn't get any response from Him. Not a single word. Consequently, His silence actually made me angrier. I thought, *After all of this turmoil, He could at least say something.* He never did.

After about a week of being in depression, crying every day, and just being mad at the world, I decided I did not want to feel this way anymore. I did not want to be depressed and I pulled myself out of it. This was on a Friday during Christmas season. We were invited to a Christmas party that night. I had originally told my husband that I did not want to go, but I called him at work and told him I changed my mind. I wanted to get out and change my scenery. I wanted to feel better. So, I got up and showered, did my nails, and got ready for the Christmas party.

Ecclesiastes 3 says, "To everything there is a season, a time for every purpose under Heaven." I believe that scripture wholeheartedly. However, I could not figure the purpose in another miscarriage. I searched and prayed, and prayed and searched. Finally, it was revealed to me. The purpose in this pregnancy was to strengthen my womb. The doctor at the in-vitro clinic told me that the lining in my uterus was too thin. Well, I beg to differ. In this last pregnancy, the baby held on to the uterine walls and would not detach himself. His attachment does not seem like a thin lining to me.

At that point I knew I could carry a child. Attachment was not an issue. Even though the doctor said one thing, I knew otherwise. My faith, my hopes, and my dreams were in tact again. God said He was going to give me a child, and the child was going to be great.

After the miscarriage many people in the church that we were attending started praying for us to have a successful pregnancy. There was one woman in particular who took a special interest in me. She was very sweet with a gentle spirit while also being uninvasive. She would gently lay a hand on my shoulder whenever she saw me and say, "I'm praying for you." I would simply reply, "Thank you. I appreciate that." For months and months she would do this, and I continued to thank her. Then one day in the summer of 2008 she said, "I have to talk to you about something. We should do lunch or something." I asked her what she needed to talk about. She replied that it was about her prayers. She said she had been on assignment from God to pray for me and she would give me the details when we got together. We exchanged numbers. I planned to call her later in the week. I kept procrastinating and procrastinating. For weeks I put it off and put it off. I was nervous to hear of what God had released her to tell me. Was it time? Was it time for me to have the long-awaited baby that He had promised? I never called her. I was just too nervous.

A couple of weeks later, I decided to hang out with my sister and a childhood friend for the weekend in Savannah. While I was away, my husband decided to visit a church in our neighborhood as opposed to going to the church we normally attend. While there, he decided to go up for altar call. After the special prayer and while he was walking back to his seat, the minister asked him to return to the altar. He walked back to the minister, not knowing why. Then the minister asked him, "Where is your wife?" He replied that I was out of town. The minister said, "Tell her that God said, 'No more.' God said, 'no more miscarriages.'" The minister then told him that when I get back, to rub anointing oil on my stomach and to pray over me.

My husband was stunned. He could not believe it. As soon as he got home he called me and told me all that happened at church. I was speechless as well. We were so excited.

When I arrived back home on Tuesday, James did exactly what the minister said. He rubbed my stomach with the oil and prayed for me. Later that night we…put faith into action.

Two weeks later, I noticed I was late. I took a pregnancy test, not thinking anything of it, and it was *positive*. I immediately remembered what the minister told my husband: "God said, 'No more miscarriages.'" I was beyond ecstatic. That same day I had a doctor's visit already scheduled for my yearly exam. I went to the appointment and immediately asked them to give me another pregnancy test. I told them that I had tested positive earlier in the day, but I just wanted to confirm. Several minutes later, the doctor, who was aware of my history, came in with a huge smile on his face. He excitedly said, "Alexis, it's positive. You're pregnant!" All I could do was smile. I had the biggest smile on my face that would not go away. The doctor then said to me, "This one is going to last. I just know it." He was so excited for me. When I got in the car, I called everyone in my family to tell them the good news. Everyone was so happy for us.

The first trimester was great. I did not have any morning sickness or any other negative symptoms. The only craving that I had was Subway sandwiches. I had them almost every day. When I was not eating a Subway sandwich, I slept the rest of the time. I promise you it was the best sleep I have ever had in my life. When I was not asleep, I used to daydream about going back to sleep. It felt so good.

Of course around the eighth week, I started to get nervous. I would worry and think, *What if I miscarry again,* but nothing happened. No spotting, not anything. It was a smooth first trimester. After the twelfth week, my fears subsided. I had made it past the timeframe of my prior miscarriages. My pregnancy was considered high risk. Therefore, the doctors scheduled a lot of checkups. From about the sixth week and going forward, I would get an ultrasound every doctor's visit, which is not common for normal pregnancies.

The second and third trimesters were uneventful. We found out at sixteen weeks that we were having a girl. We were thrilled. My husband wanted a boy like most men, but we were both happy the baby was healthy. I started to prepare more for the arrival of our little princess. Acting on faith, I decorated her room at least a year or so before I even got pregnant. For some reason I would buy all kinds of items for a baby girl. I had no idea I would have a girl one day. I just gravitated to those precious things. I even had a name for her: Ava Elizabeth. Her room was decorated in pink and green, sweet and dainty just as a baby girl would be. She had clothes in her closet and even a name plaque on the wall. It was just the letters A-V-A. Before I was pregnant, when we would have guests, they would go in the room and say things like *who is Ava* or *I didn't know you had a daughter*. I used to say that was my faith room and that God said He was going to bless me with a child. Some people would look at me strangely, but I didn't care. I just used to keep doing what I felt in my heart. Faith without works is dead.

Around thirty-four weeks, I started to get the typical swelling in my feet, which is a common symptom. When I went to the doctor, they advised me that I had early signs of preeclampsia. My blood pressure was not high enough to be classified as preeclampsia, but it was close. I was put on bed rest and they would continue to monitor the baby.

At thirty-five weeks, they noticed the baby did not grow as much as she should have in a week's period. They kept monitoring me and kept me on bed rest.

At thirty-six weeks, she did not grow at all from the previous week, so they immediately sent me to the hospital to take the baby. I was always scheduled to have a C-section, so I did not mind them taking her. I was also happy to deliver. I could not wait to meet Ava. Besides, I started to worry about her growth, and I did not want anything to go wrong. It was on Thursday, April 2, 2009. That is the day Ava was born. She was 4lbs and 15oz. She was so beautiful. I was still worried about her because she was so small in weight. The doctors and nurses kept saying to me, "We can't find one thing wrong with her. She is perfect." I was so elated. I finally had my baby.

God did it just as He said He would. It was not in my time, but it was in His time, which is the most perfect time. Ecclesiastes 3:1-2 says, "There is an appointed time for everything. And there is a time for every event under Heaven. A time to give birth and a time to die, a time to plant and a time to uproot what is planted." April 2, 2009 was the time for my little princess Ava Elizabeth Prince. It was the perfect time. It was God's time. I waited on the Lord, and He renewed my strength. I ran the race, finished, and I received the most special gift.

Life as a mom is very fulfilling. I feel complete. I do not have that void that I so longed to fill. I love her and love being her mom. She is so smart, talented, and beautiful. She loves the Lord and expresses it on a daily basis. God said that she would be great, so I am now in great anticipation of what He is going to do in her life. I thank Him every day for blessing me to be her mom.

I am thankful my prayers were answered with a pregnancy resulting in a live birth. I would be remiss if I did not speak to the many ways God could have answered my prayers. I could just as easily have adopted my Ava. Sure, she would look different and not share our DNA, but I would love her just as strong. I could have served as a mentor to several Ava's, so to speak. I would love them just as strongly.

A lot of couples are praying for a child. I cannot say couple's prayers will get answered in the way they expect. I will say to continue prayer. Ensure knowledge and work are added to faith. Lastly, keep the faith.

When I initially thought about marrying the first time, I wanted to enjoy married life like married couples that I heard about. My parents divorced when I was six, so they were not in mind when I thought of marriage. In my mind, I was going to get married and live happily ever after. It was not going to be like my parents' marriage. It was going to be like the marriage of Heathcliff and Claire from *The Cosby Show*. I am not really sure how married couples in general enjoy their lives, but my dream was to have a continuous life of love and fun like the Huxtables. I took a wary path to get to my version of the Huxtables, but thanks to God, my prince, and Ava, I have experienced a very special version.

www.ingramcontent.com/pod-product-compliance
Lightning Source LLC
Chambersburg PA
CBHW050519020526
44113CB00054B/2256